Adverbs for Advent

Adverbs for Advent

Quiet Reflections for a Noisy Time

Marilyn McEntyre

RESOURCE *Publications* · Eugene, Oregon

ADVERBS FOR ADVENT
Quiet Reflections for a Noisy Time

Resource Publications
An Imprint of Wipf and Stock Publishers
199 W. 8th Ave., Suite 3
Eugene, OR 97401

www.wipfandstock.com

PAPERBACK ISBN: 978-1-5326-4314-9
HARDCOVER ISBN: 978-1-5326-4315-6
EBOOK ISBN: 978-1-5326-4316-3

Manufactured in the U.S.A.   11/28/17

Contents

Introduction

Despite tinsel, noise, and incessant invitations to shop, the weeks of Advent are still, for many of us, a time set apart for reflection. The days on the Advent calendar are marked not only by little doors behind which small treats lie hidden but by the doors we open onto inner spaces where we may find quiet and renewal as the year draws to its end, in encounters with the indwelling Spirit.

The daily reflections in this little book (28 of them, since Advent season varies from 25 to 28 days in the liturgical calendar) are focused on the ancient question, "How, then, shall we live?" Each of them is rooted in experience, encounter, or a particular passage from Scripture or poetry that has seemed to me to address that question. They link the historical moment in which we live to the long history of faithful living and spiritual seeking that precedes us.

In this season, "the dark time of the year," may we dwell daily in light no darkness can overcome.

1

Live Generously

A dear friend and teacher offered me this last reminder as she died: "Live boldly. Live generously." She had encouraged me through many of the uncertainties of early adulthood and offered this challenging advice not as an admonition so much as an invitation to a life, I would say, a lot like hers. She modeled those virtues in the extra time she spent with struggling students (her "patients," she called them) and in the simple meals she served on a small table in her tiny apartment and in the imagination she brought to conversations that ranged from dream interpretation to the history of a Dutch river to the hidden lives of women in the rural South.

The word *generous* comes to us through medieval French where it was linked to nobility. The gentry were those who could afford to spread their wealth. The best of them believed in *noblesse oblige*—the obligation of the rich to care for the poor. To be generous in that sense means to live with an awareness of how richly we have been blessed—so richly that we can afford to spread that wealth, and should. One of the hymns I remember singing as a child proclaimed in a lusty refrain, "I'm a child of the King." It's an antique image for an abiding truth: that we are not only creatures of a divine Creator but more intimately, children of a loving God who made us dependent on each other so that in giving and receiving we might learn something of the divine life in which we're invited to participate.

The deeper root of *generous* goes back to the Latin *genus*—race or stock. That broader meaning suggests that the practice of generosity appropriately reflects our relatedness to one another as members of a human family, made from the soil (*humus*), borne in our mothers' bodies, and deeply dependent on each other and on the earth we're given to share as we learn how to be fully human.

Advent is a season set aside for recognition of God's gift of God's very self to humankind. The gifts we give one another represent not just seasonal ritual, but a reminder that we are gifts to one another and that all gifts come from and flow to an ocean of love, limitless and life-giving, utterly generous and adequate to all our needs.

2

Live Boldly

Years ago we lived across the street from a couple who had emigrated from Ireland. My daughters were amused by the occasional scolding the mother gave her more mischievous child: "You're a bold girl!" They laughed because the word had such a different meaning in the stories we read at home about bold adventurers or bold and courageous deeds. But the Irish usage opened a nice occasion for reflection on the double-edged virtue of boldness.

Little Carrie's "boldness" was often rooted in curiosity that took her beyond prescribed boundaries and got her into awkward, sometimes dangerous situations. She was "bold" when something mattered more to her in the moment than remembering rules and warnings. She tried things. She got into trouble.

But trouble, of course, is what heroes and adventurers get into as well. The bold ones break rules—not for the sake of breaking them, but because they're following a call, a star, a guide, an urge, a love that takes them to a wider place where love is law and legalism gives way to a deeper, steadier, sturdier, more personal consent to a summoning. Jesus' bold responses to the literal-minded keepers of the law are the best reminders of what it means to live boldly: to remember what the law is for and from whom it came, to break it when a higher law applies, to listen for guidance and pray for clarity and then act.

We need boldness now, this year, this season. To protect those who are threatened by guns and deportation and climate change, to speak truth to those abusing power, to care for water and soil and ecosystems, for other species and their fragile habitats requires boldness in identifying and acting against greed—our own and others'.

Advent meditations direct us toward inwardness. It is "the dark time of the year" when burrowing and quieting, pondering and preparing are liturgically thematic. But all that preparation is for a purpose, which *The Presbyterian Book of Common Worship* articulates boldly: "Go out into the world in peace; have courage; hold on to what is good; return no one evil for evil; strengthen the fainthearted; support the weak, and help the suffering; honor all people; love and serve the Lord, rejoicing in the power of the Holy Spirit." It's an invigorating charge and an invitation to dare punishment, if need be, to follow the Spirit's summons, even into streets and city councils and policy debates and places of squalid poverty—and even into the heart of our own homes where life-sustaining work sometimes requires the uncomfortable conversations that keep the way open for Love.

3

Live Vigilantly

I learned the term "hypervigilance" from a psychologist whose practice was full of adults who had learned habits of fear as children. They had lived on high alert because an unpredictable or abusive parent might strike out at any time, or because an adult's anxiety made every situation seem fraught with dire possibilities. Hypervigilance is an all-too-common pathology—tragic in children and crippling in adults who haven't found healing.

Vigilance, on the other hand, is an invigorating, life-sustaining quality shared by those whose instinct and training is to protect. "Be sober, be watchful," we read in the liturgy for compline, "for your adversary the devil goes about like a roaring lion, seeking whom he may devour" (1 Peter 5:8). Some translations substitute "vigilant" for "watchful." I like that rendering, since it recalls the sacred practice of keeping vigil as so many have done as they sit with the dying, pray through the night before a significant feast day or impending crisis, stand outside prisons in silent protest lines, holding candles. The original meaning of the word includes not only watchfulness, but staying awake, being lively or active, staying strong. It's a rich term for the kind of watchfulness that is full of intention and whole-hearted intelligence.

As political turbulence continues in this country and around the world, many people feel a heightened sense of danger. Muslims, migrants, people living at social and economic margins, people dependent on under-funded public services, children who internalize the half-understood fears of their elders are on higher alert. Those of us who don't belong to targeted, mistreated, or traumatized populations can keep vigil with them, watching the signs of the times, considering specifically and locally what protection might look like, increasing giving to organizations that provide legal assistance, crisis care or simple acts of friendship and solidarity in public places when harassment happens.

It was heartening to read a while back of the response of store staff and customers to public harassment of a Muslim woman: when they heard the shouting, people emerged from all over the store to stand with her, make sure she was safe as she bought her groceries, and walk her to the car. Awake, aware, and willing to act, they provided me with a valuable image of what it means to live vigilantly so that the vulnerable need not fall into chronic anxiety and hypervigilance.

Watching out for each other, noticing what needs to be noticed, waiting actively rather than passively for institutional changes and policy reform, and certainly watching over the little ones who are facing adult problems too soon, protecting their safety and their childhood, are good ways of keeping vigil, as the ancients did, "on the eve of a religious festival," as an act of devotion to the God in whom we can, even in the midst of trouble, find our peace.

4

Live Attentively

I recently saw a father stop in the aisle of a hardware store, lay down the tool he was considering, squat to his child's eye level and listen to whatever it was the little boy had to say. It may have been simply one of the tedious "Can we go now?" queries every parent hears from children who are tired of trekking around on adult business. It may have been a request to stop for a snack on the way home. Or it may have been a feeling he'd never have shared if he hadn't had a parent who was likely to listen.

That dad's attentiveness came as a reminder in the midst of my own busy morning to slow down and pay attention. I was eager to leave; hardware stores are not my favorite places to spend time, especially looking for specific sizes of screws or exchanging the wrong drill bits for the right ones.

I love the history of the word "attentive." The Latin, *adtendere*, means to stretch toward. When we are attentive we extend ourselves—we direct our gaze, we incline our ear, we may lean toward or step into or offer a hand or a shoulder or a lap. The French *attendre* generally means "wait," or sometimes, as an imperative, something like our colloquial "Listen up!" In the highly ceremonial Byzantine Catholic services I've attended with awe and deep pleasure, the Bible is lifted high before the Gospel reading and all are summoned to listen more closely with the words, "Wisdom! Be attentive!"

Attentiveness not only opens us to wisdom, it is its own practice of wisdom. Anyone who has known me for a while will have heard me quote musician Roberto Gerhard's words, which I kept on the wall during the months I worked on my dissertation, and which have, many times since, helped me return from distraction to a place of attentiveness: "Attention—deep, sustained, undeviating—is, in itself, an experience of a very high order." I love even the commas in that sentence, and the dashes—the way they slow the eye down and invite you to pause over each word—to go in before going on. Attentive is slow. And spacious. Leaning in, ready to act, but poised and pausing to notice the density and texture and complexity of the moment. As one hymn writer described God: "Unresting, unhasting, and silent as light." May the quality of the attention we give be a little more like that in this season of celebrating light that shines in the darkness and is not overcome.

5

Live Imaginatively

My favorite question asked of men and women preparing for ordination in the Presbyterian Church is this: "Will you seek to serve the people with energy, intelligence, imagination, and love?" The question reminds both the person being ordained and those who count on pastors for competent, faithful leadership that each of those qualities matters. It's not enough to be theologically educated. Or to be committed to church growth or to programs or even to good preaching. The habits of mind and heart the question identifies challenge the person entering leadership to understand service as a matter of ongoing spiritual development, and the vocation of ministry as an ongoing process of seeking.

I've come to believe that imagination is one of the human qualities most encouraged in Scripture—especially in the Gospels. The parables might well begin with "Imagine this . . . ." Imagine what it feels like to be the man lying by the side of the road who has to accept help from a member of an enemy tribe. Or imagine the distress of a woman who has lost a coin she needs for household expenses. Or of a father whose son has rebelled, wasted his inheritance, and held his father's hopes in contempt. Imagine the kingdom of heaven not as a political triumph or an equitable economic system but as a mustard seed or a leavened loaf or a wedding banquet. Imagine, when you walk urban streets, what it is like to be homeless or chronically hurried or culturally displaced or disoriented and scared.

The biblical story is riddled with gaps that leave room for imagination, reminding us that Scripture is not an instruction book, but a story to be entered as a place of habitation and exploration, a story that provides maps and clues and equipment for our unique journeys. Story after story in Old and New Testaments tease us into imagining: how did Sarah feel when Abraham and Isaac returned from their traumatic, transformative moment on the mountain? What did Joseph say when Mary told him she was with child? What happened to Lazarus after he was raised from the dead? What did Jesus do on his long sojourns in the desert? How did sudden sight change the blind man's life? We are left to imagine.

If we enter those gaps and dwell there, imagination will become a habit, and we will begin to see each other and the circumstances of our shared lives with eyes more open to possibilities. The most imaginative people I've known don't pass quick or unthinking judgment. They don't stereotype. They are more compassionate because they can imagine their way into others' points of view, constraints, problems, hopes, histories.

It has seemed to me over decades of teaching literature that the main reason to read fiction or poems or plays is to foster compassion. And peacemaking. The wise reminder that "The only peace we can have is the peace we can imagine" challenges us all to put real energy into imagining, as specifically as possible, what peace might look like. Out of that inner work come changed behavior, new strategies, courage to change what we can, the wisdom to focus our efforts effectively. Imaginative living is playful and trusting, engaged and engaging, capable of going to very dark places, and of delight in ordinary things. It's a good way to live. We're designed for it. And called to it.

6

Live Healthily

Every faith community carries some wisdom other people of faith can learn from—a style of worship or focus in ministry or way of understanding Spirit or scripture that may complement or correct our own. I've found myself this year especially grateful for the way Seventh Day Adventists practice and teach healthy eating as a dimension of spiritual life. Vegetarian eating is one of the commitments they're probably best known for by folks who know little else about their theology and shared practices. They also avoid alcohol, tobacco, and caffeine. The ones I've met are not rigid about these guidelines, but believe, as one of their websites says, that "God calls us to care for our bodies, treating them with the respect a divine creation deserves." Collectively, over a period of long shared conversation, they have arrived at a common understanding of what caring for bodies looks like.

There are plenty of references to eating meat in scripture. Jesus fried up fish with the disciples even after the Resurrection. So it's easy enough to quibble about vegetarianism. I think it's a good idea, but that's not my point at present. Rather I find myself reflecting on eating and the life of the spirit. The clearest connection between healthy eating practices and spiritual life is that we are stewards of our bodies, reminded to remember that they are "temples of the Holy Spirit" and we are keepers and inhabitants of those temples.

I like the simple reminder, "Eat to live; don't live to eat." Eating to live seems to me to be one practical, earthy way of claiming the promise that we who follow the way Jesus opened will have life, and have it abundantly. Eating to live involves paying attention to what foods in fact do enhance life, energy and clarity and what foods (or artificial food-like-substances), on the other hand, clog the system and induce sluggishness or cravings or addiction.

Advent, since it is not only a sacred season in the church year but also a season of frenzied shopping and eating, seems a good time to embrace physical health as a dimension of faithful living. And perhaps to watch a good food documentary: *Fed Up*, for instance, or *Forks Over Knives*, or *Food Stamped* or *Food, Inc.* or the edgier *What the Health*. Or to read Michael Pollen's inspiring *In Defense of Food* or Jon Robbins' *Diet for a New World* or Jonathan Foer's stirring personal story about food and conscience, *Eating Animals*. These works all focus widely and compassionately not only on personal but also on public health as a matter for ongoing ethical reflection. They're not offensively doctrinaire, but encouraging and heartening: living healthily lifts up the heart, enlivens community, and readies us to undertake whatever is given us to do with "energy, intelligence, imagination and love." *Bon appetit.*

7

Live Beautifully

I suppose Henry James is an acquired taste. It's one I acquired some years ago with the help of a wry and wonderful literature professor who fully understood why so many find James' writing tedious and unreadable. Since then I've idled with surprising pleasure over the long sentences that thicken his novels which can, admittedly, border on excess. One critic observed dryly that James "chewed more than he bit off." I've also come to appreciate his peculiar use of adverbs that frequently offer startling angles of vision, the way just one brush stroke of an unlikely color can change a painting. One he seemed particularly fond of was "beautifully." He described characters' actions as "beautifully" carried out, or their thoughts as "beautifully" apt. One character, by his simplicity and honesty, makes another's efforts to probe his motives "beautifully irrelevant." James stretches the word to include a sense of precision, timeliness, and deftness, suggesting also that what is beautiful is perfectly fitting to the occasion.

"Live beautifully" is the kind of advice I would expect from James' characters, and from the man himself, who understood that beauty was a form of goodness. It took time, and kind and insightful teachers, to release me from the vaguely suspicious approach to art, theater, and any but natural beauty that came with the evangelical iconoclasm I grew up in. Though I still admire and cherish the ethic of simplicity embodied in Thoreau's *Walden*, and in the lives of the Amish or the Mennonites or the Quakers—their bare, open spaces, their quiet, their plain speech—I also recognize that for me, and perhaps for most of us, the hunger for beauty runs deep. The deep purple of Van Gogh's wild irises, the sorrow expressed in Michelangelo's Roman pietà, the conversation between violin and cello in Schubert's Quintet in C Major can open the heart and teach it tenderness or patience or awe.

Part of our work in the world, part of the love we're here to learn and share, is to make sure that what is beautiful is cared for—the oak groves, the glistening fish, the rose windows, the tribal masks, the conversation of children. And, since access to beauty is undeniably a measure of privilege, it behooves us to make sure that beauty is made accessible to those who live in squalor—not always the poor, but also those who, entrapped in soulless commercial landscapes, need contact with the best that "earth has given and human hands have made."

To live beautifully is essentially to do what Mother Teresa urged: to do small things with great love—setting the table, lighting Advent candles, washing windows to make the winter branches more visible in morning light. And it is to live as a grateful recipient of the light that surrounds us and teaches us, as Emerson put it, that "all things glitter and swim."

8

Live Simply

"Simplicity, patience, compassion. These three are your greatest treasures." "Our life is frittered away by detail. Simplify, simplify." "All the fun is there, in the simple life!" "Less is more." "Live simply that others may simply live." "Consider the lilies of the field . . . ." Every faith tradition and a wide range of secular writers teach the wisdom of simplicity. The popularity of periodicals like *Simple Living* and *Yes!* and of books like *The Life-Changing Magic of Tidying Up*, *Voluntary Simplicity*, *Choosing Simplicity*, and *Animal, Vegetable, Miracle* testifies to how many of us long for a little less.

Every year, though I welcome Advent as a season of reflection and hope, I also regard its approach with a certain ambivalence. The tide of ads beginning before "Black Friday" rises to a tsunami even as Advent candles burn. Hospitality, festivity and travel to and from family folk are good and fitting impulses but also fraught with organizational complications and detail and expense. This year the season also comes in the wake of a political upheaval which, for all its ominous effects, has also involved us in a much-needed conversation about climate-change, privilege, overconsumption, and the radical inequities of a polarized economy. It's not a simple conversation, nor a comfortable one. This is a season that unsettles the conscience and invites us to take a long look at our hopes and habits.

It's a good time to clean out the garage and contribute to the local coat drive. It's a good time to reread the Sermon on the Mount and remember the rich young ruler. It's a good time to read Wendell Berry and Bill McKibben and even pull *Walden* down off the shelf where it may have been gathering dust with *The Norton Anthology* and other reminders of old English classes. Each of these writers helps keep me accountable: they encourage me to keep asking myself hard questions about what I buy, what my dollars support, and what difference my eating habits make to the health of the earth.

Some of these arise in the aisles of stores, some as I prepare meals, some as I read *The New York Times*: How can I be generous and also prudent? Hospitable and also contemplative? Hopeful and also realistic about the threats we face? Broad in my sympathies and focused in my efforts to take effective action? How can I respond to the urgencies around me and also live simply, quietly, thoughtfully, locally, kindly, making space for each encounter and for the prayer and meditation without which I have so little of value to offer?

These are not questions that lend themselves to simple answers, though they direct me toward the ideal and ethic of simplicity Jesus preached and embodied and inspired. They do serve to keep me in a place of ongoing discernment and help me to look at the calendar a little more calmly. I don't need rules (though St. Benedict's *Rule* is helpful). I need to stay attuned to the Spirit who is available when I ask: Is this a moment to give or to withhold? Is this a call to offer an extra measure of kindness or to protect myself from squandering my energies? Is this a time to wade into complex, emotionally fraught negotiations or to remain quiet and return to center?

Moment by moment we receive the guidance we need. Praying without ceasing is essentially a matter of staying tuned in. Living simply, I have come to believe, is largely a matter of asking, and then listening for instruction about what to take on and what to leave alone, and for what purpose, and for whose sake. And then acting with "gladness and singleness of heart."

9

Live Expectantly

We live in an unfolding story. The plot thickens and turns. If we look back, we can see patterns emerging—themes, intersections, loops, roads not taken. The mystery and paradox of Advent lie in its emphasis on expectation: believers wait in "sure and certain hope" that what has happened will happen. What has been true will be true again, new every year, yet still to come, fact and promise. We live, as theologians put it, in the "already but not yet." In cold, candle-lit churches people gather and sing, "Come, thou long-expected Jesus," remembering an ancient birth, awaiting a new one, hoping against hope.

The word *expect* took an interesting turn in its journey from first-century Latin to 21st century English: before 1600 it was commonly used to mean "wait" or "defer action." Only later did it acquire its current meaning of "await" or "desire, hope, long for, look for with anticipation." Vestiges of the older meaning make the word a kind of palimpsest—a reused manuscript on which traces of earlier inscription remain. To live expectantly is to live in hope—even in longing—but also to wait patiently for what will happen in due time. Or, to put it biblically, "in the fullness of time."

Expectation as a state of mind and spirit is not only a large, eschatological idea; it may also be a daily practice and habit of mind. To live expectantly is to know something is afoot. The Spirit, who watches over, broods and guides and blows where it will, may any moment show up or show forth. If we are willing to notice, we will notice how apparent coincidences, unplanned encounters, and even obstacles work as invitations or nudges or reminders or directives.

It is possible to live expectantly without insisting on or even nam-ing what we expect. It is possible to "look for with anticipation" without a particular object in mind, like a child without a Christmas list (a dwindling remnant) for whom the unopened package promises utter surprise. Simply to expect that we will be given what we need for our growth, that we will be invited again and again to awaken, pay attention, learn, stretch into love in new ways, practice discernment, exercise generosity, or rest and be held, is a rich and joyous way of life.

T.S. Eliot's mysterious admonishment in "Little Gidding," " . . . wait without hope / For hope would be hope for the wrong thing," cautions against fixing our hopes on objects of our own feeble imagining rather than waiting, hoping, and expecting an end to the unfolding story, or the next plot twist, that we cannot fully imagine. Despite the hard political facts, despite ecological and economic anxieties, we can take heart in the habit of expectation--that there will be a new heaven and a new earth, that help will come for us all, trailing "clouds of glory," and that the day will offer gifts and surprises and answers to questions we didn't know to ask.

10

Live Wholeheartedly

When he was two or three, my grandson Matthew, now a skilled gymnast, would throw his whole body onto sofas, beds, piles of pillows, grassy slopes, or, sometimes, his large, patient dog in moments of complete delight. His heedless abandon was a little nerve-wracking to witness, though he rarely hurt himself. But the sheer physical joy he took in leaping, landing, rolling and laughing was a pleasure for all of us less daring onlookers.

I remember Matthew's flying leaps when I think of the line in Ecclesiastes, "Whatsoever your hand finds to do, do it with your might." Somehow, I misremembered the ending of that verse for a long time as ". . . do it with your whole heart." That paraphrase helps me a bit more than "might," but both serve to remind me to refocus and re-center when I'm mired in ambivalence, second-guessing myself, or distracting myself with concerns about what I'm not doing rather than attending to the task at hand.

The road not taken, the unanswered letters, the friends one is not seeing can always impinge on the moment. (As my husband is fond of quoting, to make the point, "If you're reading Dostoevsky you're not playing the cello.") It is a discipline to bring one's whole heart to each encounter or each task, to release oneself wholeheartedly into meditation or prayer or rest, to consent fully and willingly to the call of the moment or to make one's "No" as clear and unambiguous as possible, because clarity is a gift, even when it disappoints.

I remember years ago attending a friend's party when I was too tired, too burdened by other obligations, too short on time, and in no mood to be sociable. Despite what I thought were my best efforts, she noticed. "It feels as if you don't want to be here," she said in her forthright but kindly non-judgmental way. She was right. I wanted to honor the occasion, so I had made myself come, but my reluctant presence was no great gift to her or anyone else that afternoon. A loving note in which I wholeheartedly expressed my honest affection would have been, on that occasion, the better choice.

I was inclined then, and am still, to reiterate for emphasis, but a wise friend offered me the curious advice, "Two things you should say only once: 'I'm sorry' and 'Thank you.'" I thought long about that, since I tend to underscore both apologies and thanks with repetition. His rule suggests that when forgiveness or thanks are wholehearted—genuine and deeply felt, holding nothing back—speaking them once will confer the blessing intended. Repetition can add nothing to a true and wholehearted word.

Wholeness of heart, like health, is a blessing, and it confers blessing. It radiates. It gives words weight. It is a stay against deception. And it magnifies every kindness.

11

Live Prudently

Now there's an unpopular word. Sounds a little like *prune* or *prude*. Puritans used to name their daughters Prudence. It's not hard to imagine what middle-schoolers now would do to those hapless girls. But I learned in graduate school to appreciate the social, musical, and emotional complexity of Puritan culture from a lively and wonderful scholar who enabled us to imagine people who might actually find something lovely and lifegiving in the virtue of prudence.

The word comes from the Latin *providencia*, which meant foresight or the wisdom to see ahead and act with informed discretion. We, of course, get our word *providence* from that—provision and care that comes from wise oversight. One dictionary also explains that prudence is the "wisdom to see what is suitable or profitable." It is practical wisdom about how to live well in the world and justly (consider the term jurisprudence).

Elinor Dashwood, the character from Jane Austen's *Sense and Sensibility* memorably played by Emma Thompson in the 1995 film version of that remarkable novel, embodies prudence and offers good reason to reflect on this undersung virtue. (I urge both the book and the film upon you, dear reader, in that order.) Compared to her more romantic, more expressive, more appealing, but sadly less prudent, sister Marianne, Elinor seems a bit pale at first—understated, a little too reasonable, a little less fun. Yet she has her passions, humor, and wit that are a delight to discover, appetite for life and pleasure in what is truly beautiful. She emerges as a woman comparable to Shakespeare's similarly prudent Portia in whom intellect and largeness of heart combine to give us a vivid image of grace.

I especially like the way the literal meaning of the root word, foresight, links prudence to a wider perspective, a capacity to see what is unfolding and to imagine implications and consequences of the moment's choices. Foresight suggests a habit of mind that connects the dots—a capacity to imagine how one thing might lead to another, where plot complications might arise, what circumstances might prove to be mitigating. It lies at the heart of what some have called "moral intelligence."

To live prudently would be to ask the "how" and "what if" and "wherefore" questions that give pause. It would be to forego the momentary pleasure of leaping to comfortable conclusions or giving way to a wild impulse. It does not come easily to the impatient. But to slow is not to stop. The slowing of a prudent mind allows time to take in the complexity of all choices, of others' needs or one's own, of the historical moment, the political quandary, the professional tradeoffs.

And I don't think prudence forecloses entirely the joy of those "wild and precious" moments when we are called to act on intuition or a sudden summoning of the Spirit without long deliberation. The discernment it takes to know those moments when they come may be exactly where the wisdom of a prudent mind is most rewarding: to release oneself into the wave, onto the ski slope, or the wind current or the wide, smooth ice, trusting the body and the elements is a joy that comes most fully to those who, prudently, have trained and taken instruction and so prepared themselves for the fullness of delight.

12

Live Globally

Two of our dear friends get up every day and read *Al Jazeera* along with *The New York Times*. Another gets his morning news from the British-based *Guardian*, another from *Der Spiegel*, and another from *The Independent*, because Robert Fisk seems to him one of the most reliable journalists alive. We feel that way about Amy Goodman, whose commitment to showing up in dangerous places and reporting stories or points of view that are omitted or underrepresented on networks controlled by large corporate interests make her a partner of the poor as well as a champion of human rights. Her news hour, *Democracy Now!*, has regularly featured victims of natural and humanitarian catastrophes around the world, whistleblowers, soldiers whose boots have been "on the ground" and who live with the PTSD that is a common cost of war. I have set my homepage to *commondreams.org*, a source that similarly stays free of commercial sponsorship and hosts thoughtful discussion of global issues. These are only a handful among the many providers of global perspectives that are so important now, living as we do in a world where national boundaries mean less and less in the face of climate change, multinational corporations, and resource interdependence.

The bumper-sticker advice (and there's plenty of it on the highways I travel) to "Think Globally, Act Locally" seems to me more important as the months go by. Even though a lot of us suffer periodic spasms of "information anxiety" and news overload, it matters to know that courageous doctors without borders are working among people in war zones who are trapped without food, water, or adequate medical care; that indigenous people in Mexico, the Philippines, Ecuador, Nigeria, and the US are working with nonprofits to protect land and water from the effects of aggressive oil extraction; that Paul Botoman, the "borehole doctor," has repaired wells in 140 villages in Malawi with the help of water.org, quietly saving lives and livelihoods.

We can't each know all the news—bad or good—but we can widen our imaginations and compassion and sense of relatedness to others who share the planet. We can connect the dots—not that many of them—that lead from our kitchen tables to the coffee fields in Columbia or the olive groves in Israel-Palestine or the rice paddies in Vietnam. We can remember that a dollar spent is a vote for a process and do what we can to make sure we are involved in just and sustainable processes. We can go to where we will meet immigrants and hear their stories, show up at fundraisers for just causes, and do the homework required to understand the complexities of the issues being addressed.

We were all sent here on assignment. This earth is our common home (and I highly recommend the documentary simply entitled *Home* to help deepen our understanding of that truth) and its inhabitants our fellow travelers. Advent is a good time for adventure; we can venture into new places on earth without leaving much of a carbon footprint by plugging into public conversation and learning from each other how to help heal broken systems and broken hearts, giving thanks, always for the beauty of the earth.

13

Live Locally

I know people who have lived all their lives in one place. I'm not one of them. I've moved from one coast to the other and up and down California in my peregrinations, sometimes looking with envy at those who have done less packing and more planting. Either, of course can be "a path with a heart."

The adage sometimes attributed to Confucius, "Wherever you go, there you are," offers an oddly tautological reminder to pause regularly, look around, take stock, and engage with those we encounter—family or strangers. Be local. Be a neighbor. Wrench yourself away from the internet, take a walk, and find out what's happening (including among non-human creatures), who's making it happen, who's being affected, and how to help. That might mean reading the announcements in the church bulletin and showing up to pack lunches for the homeless. It might mean signing up to tutor reading at a school where kids are struggling. It might mean making your home a welcoming place for neighborhood meetings or cub scouts or a grief group. Or introducing yourself to those you encounter on a walk through the park. It might mean buying from local businesses or filling your bags at the local farmer's market.

That last option has especially wide implications: eating local food contributes, meal by meal, to reducing our dependence on the "petroleum-drenched" food that travels an average of 1500 miles to our tables, leaving a large carbon footprint and perpetuating forms of farming that are by and large unsustainable. Eating locally means we can get to know some of the people who bring the food to our table, for whom we often pray as we begin a meal—so many of them—the CSA farmers who are quietly, laboriously expanding the market for sustainable, organic food--the sturdy folks who set up booths at markets on weekends and chat with customers, the people who introduce us to cherimoyas, kohlrabi and other vegetable outliers, the neighbors who bring free lemons to meetings or distribute zucchini to anyone who will take it at the end of summer.

Living locally means being aware of process, which, mostly, we aren't. We don't know the people who made our computers or pajamas or IKEA furniture. But we do know who made the brownies being sold at the school fund-raiser and the casseroles to which we add our own in homes where someone has recently died. And we know that person's name. And can offer hugs to the one who is left, weeping. And we weep with them. Because their lives also belong to us, if we are their neighbors—a word whose biblical sense is deep and capacious. "Who is my neighbor" is one of the great, significant questions in the Gospels. If someone nearby were to ask it, the answer would surely have to be, "I am."

14

Live Playfully

Peter Matthiessen's lovely title, *At Play in the Fields of the Lord*, rings a happy change on the metaphor that motivated hundreds of Christian missionaries to venture into foreign lands and cultures, understanding themselves as laborers in the fields of the Lord. I grew up with my parents' memories of years working "on the mission field" in India, not recognizing the term as an agricultural metaphor until well into adult life. Those same kindly parents took me to prayer meetings where we occasionally sang the nineteenth-century hymn "Work for the Night is Coming," based on John 9:4: "As long as it is day, I must do the work of him that sent me. Night is coming, when no one can work."

The emphasis on working, laboring, expending one's energies in God's service, is part of a legacy I still value, misdirected though some of those energies have been, where evangelism has been entangled with colonialism and tainted by often unconscious racism. That work ethic, no doubt, accounts for my father's frequent query as we sat on the floor playing Monopoly, "Why aren't you doing something useful?" And my mother's cheerful measure of her days on this earth: "Honey, when I'm not useful any more, I just want to go." They were faithful people and not without their own kind of playfulness and humor, but it wasn't until early adulthood that I came to appreciate play also as a calling. The Lord's fields might be places where one could toss a ball around or play tag.

David James Duncan's title, *God Laughs and Plays*, was worth the price of the book to me before I even opened its rich, provocative, insightful pages. Subtitled "Churchless Sermons in Response to the Preachments of the Fundamentalist Right," the book is a gathering of sermons and talks that reclaim God's image and the Gospel's message from those who have darkened it with human judgment and stringent moral strictures—including an overwrought work ethic. The playfulness of Duncan's prose, and of Annie Dillard's and of Billy Collins' poetry and even of Emily Dickinson's, offers a sprightly, inspiring reminder that play is a form of intelligence. It is also a form of thanksgiving, and of praise, and of fidelity. With respect to that fidelity, Stephen Nachmanovich writes in *Free Play*, "When we are totally faithful to our own individuality, we are actually following a very intricate design." Play is a response to a summons we all receive: discover who you are, where your curiosities lead you, what gives you life and joy, and what lies within you waiting to be brought forth.

As I grow older I recognize that the people I have most admired and learned from are all playful people. They experiment. They receive the "spur of the moment" and respond. They try out alternative points of view. They pretend for the sheer pleasure of peering down a road not taken. And their capacity for intense, focused, productive work is sustained by the wisdom that allows them to suspend that work for a whole afternoon while they throw a ball around with a ten-year-old or hide behind trees waiting to be found, or sit cross-legged on the floor in front of a game board, caring less about the outcome than about the little opponents for whom this competition has the look of love.

15

Live Faithfully

"Love changes, and in change is true," Wendell Berry writes in his lovely poem, "The Dance." The line articulates what most recognize who have maintained long, loving relationships with spouses, friends, children. Faithfulness is a much more nuanced and lively virtue than simply sticking with or sticking to or sticking it out. It is much more like what John Ciardi describes in his poem, "Men Marry What They Need: I Marry You":

> . . . I marry you,
> morning by morning, day by day, night by night,
> and every marriage makes this marriage new.

That kind of faithful living is more "again and again" than "on and on"— saying an intentional yes that is new every morning.

In his collection of stories entitled *Fidelity* Berry explores a rich variety of ways in which people are faithful to one another. A daughter visits her father in prison when he has, in a fit of rage, killed a much beloved friend. A man notices his wife's unspoken need and quietly finds ways to meet it, surprising her into recognizing that what she needed was there all along. A soldier returns home, traumatized, but prepared to find the healing he needs among people he trusts. A young man, against hospital regulations, steals a beloved older man who has been a father to him and the community from the hospital where he doesn't want to die, and takes him to a familiar rural spot where dying can really be a going home. A couple of men save neighbors from a flood. In each story the main characters are faithful not simply to an abstract notion of moral obligation, but to what they know by long experience to be needful in the moment. Faithfulness like that is a kind of knowledge.

Most of us, if we've lived long enough, have been unfaithful in small things, if not in big ones. Living faithfully, more than a matter of good record, is a matter of grateful and trusting return through a door that is never locked against us when we have "erred and strayed"—accepting God's great faithfulness, repenting, and beginning again. Faithfulness is also a matter of growing in clarity about what we hope to be faithful to—a vocation, a way of seeing, an agreement, a relationship, and choosing it against all competing distractions. And choosing again: when life changes the terms, reframing those choices and returning to yes.

16

Live Gratefully

One of the many things I find endearing about my husband is that he thanks me when I do the most ordinary things—roll up the socks, sort the mail, pick up the groceries I always pick up. Kale again—thank you. Some of the tasks I do for our mutual wellbeing are simply my part of a fair distribution of labor, part of the rhythm of shared life, not unusual gestures of kindness, simply doing my part, as he does his. But thanking each other for small things has, I think, added an extra dimension of happiness to a happy marriage.

Gratitude is a practice, a habit of the heart, an orientation, a way of seeing, a form of wisdom. A lot has been written and said about cultivating an "attitude of gratitude," identifying five things a day to be grateful for, and even understanding gratitude from a scientific point of view. Here, for instance, are a few websites that offer a range of cheering reminders of the goodness of gratitude: *happify.com; unstuck.com; tinybuddha.com; lifehack. org; stratejoy.com; spiritualityhealth.com; thechangeblog.com; productive- muslim.com; explorefaith.org.* Christians, Buddhists, Muslims, Hindus and other faith groups as well as many who claim no particular faith have gone public in praise of this life-giving practice.

Identifying what we are grateful for is, indeed, a valuable way of noticing, as we go along, how much of life is given, and gift. How much we receive without our own efforts, from the generosity of others' labor and of the abundant earth and of the Creator who spoke it all into being and holds it as it struggles and evolves. And gratitude is a good antidote to discouragement, depression, cynicism, and even despair—things many feel particularly acutely during the holiday season, and some especially this

31

year as political havoc has raised so many deeply unsettling questions about our life together.

But an archaeology of gratitude can also take us beyond helpful habit to deep, existential layers of self-understanding that remind us that life itself is a gift, that we live and move in mystery, that perhaps gratitude is a foundational grasp of who we are and how we are to live. That two basic instructions for growing into the lives we've been given are simply these: "Say yes. Say thank you." We may leave the "you" in that sentence open wide to imaging and interpretation, but that thanks is due is a matter of remarkable agreement among most of us when we are being our most humble, human, and humane.

17

Live Mercifully

It was only after I memorized Portia's lovely speech for Mrs. Matson, my exacting senior English teacher, that I learned the actual meaning of its first line: "The quality of mercy is not strain'd." "Strained" meant "forced or constrained," and the line insists simply that mercy cannot be wrung from God or others by force but must be freely given. No law compels a judge or an adversary to be merciful: the law is about justice. Mercy transcends justice when it "droppeth as the gentle rain from heaven upon the place beneath," blessing "him that gives and him that takes." Though *The Merchant of Venice* is a troubling play sullied by a distressing strain of anti-Semitism, its famous reminder of the wisdom of mercy still presents an eloquent appeal to reach beyond an ethic of strict justice to a wider, more generous understanding of what we need from God and each other.

But mercy can't be constrained, as any parent knows who has tried to appeal to a small child to get beyond "That's not fair!" and understand that the offending playmate may be hurting or sad. It's a delicate business: "fair" is a good standard to hold on to. We want children to learn to be fair. There can be no mercy without justice: socially, legally, and psychologically, justice comes first. Debt forgiveness assumes mutual recognition that a debt is owed. A sentence can be commuted only if a sentence has been pronounced, and a commuted sentence doesn't pretend that the judgment was wrong—only that a greater good may be served by extending mercy.

I have depended on other people's mercy when I have disappointed or failed them. I am among the many who can sing with conviction that I'm "standin' in the need of prayer," and in need of gracious, imaginative understanding. Because of that I have come to believe that the only way to be truly merciful is to recognize how often and undeservedly I have received mercy. I can afford to give what I have so abundantly received.

In Exodus—another unsettling story—the Lord says, "I will have mercy on whom I will have mercy," insisting that divine generosity is not to be limited by any human notion of justice, or by any human measure of "just desserts."

Mercy is not rational. It is wisdom of the heart, not of the mind. And, as Portia points out, "earthly power doth then show likest God's when mercy seasons justice." Mercy is, in a sense, a privilege of the powerful. To live mercifully is to recognize our own empowerment as children of God, as free agents, as the fortunate who have been "twice blessed." And to recognize also how we need mercy from the oppressed from whom our privilege has been stolen.

Portia's appeal to Shylock may be misdirected. But it widens where she reminds him that "in the course of justice, none of us should see salvation." For that brief moment she aligns herself and all those she defends with the one among them who has been so despised. It is a flicker of the solidarity that is called for in seasons of political hostilities, deportations, xenophobia, threats, and fear. Mercy for those whom the law condemns where the law has not served them well, mercy for those who have crossed borders in the dead of night to save their lives, mercy also for those whose political positions we find incomprehensible, even as we oppose them, because we are in no position to judge their motivations: none of these can be constrained. But it may be in these varieties of mercy that we find our way through to a peace we can only begin again to imagine.

18

Live Patiently

Among the things a poet must depend on, according to Wendell Berry in his poem "How to Be a Poet" is "patience, / for patience joins time / to eternity." I'm not entirely sure what he means by the rather abstract idea that patience joins time to eternity, except that it reminds me that God has time. And in the order of creation, things take time to unfold in their appointed ways.

Among the many instructions to the faithful in the book of James we encounter this curious reiteration: ". . . be patient. Establish your hearts . . . ." In biblical texts *establish* is mostly used with reference to covenants or laws; they are announced and agreed upon, inscribed, even set in stone. We also see it in the prayer that God would "establish the work of our hands"— make it fixed, stable, lasting. Establishing anything requires time. It takes time to travel the learning curve, form habits, be shaped by the gentle pressure of practice.

Patience, like prudence, seems one of the less glamorous virtues, perhaps because it seems so passive; it's easily confused with, say, putting up with. Or waiting it out. One can imagine settling in for a long wait with a sigh or even a roll of the eyes. But I think patience deserves better press.

Real patience isn't passive, but active: waiting patiently requires not just endurance but imagination. If you are really capable of patience you can imagine how it might take weeks for a broken bone to repair itself, or months for a baby to prepare for birth, or years for a forest to restore itself after a fire. You can empathize with a child's or a puppy's impulse to dawdle along on a walk, sniffing and examining and pausing to watch a hummingbird or a hawk. You can slow your own pace for the sake of seeing what they do, choosing against your own urgency and haste.

On this day of Advent I want to celebrate the patience of my teachers, whose gentle reiterations cost them, I know, time that might have been spent more enjoyably elsewhere. And of the nurses and doctors who have seen me through healing, unwilling to hurry the process. And of a spouse who has the good grace to laugh when I take more time than he would getting out the door. Their patience has shown me a dimension of love that, like a facet on a diamond, shows forth a startling color that waits to be revealed.

19

Live Deliberately

It's a question I ask a child when another child has hurt her in some minor way: "Do you think he did it deliberately?" It's a question juries are bound to consider. It's a word often used with reference to misconduct. But deliberation is a powerful practice and a good measure of maturity.

The original root word was *librare*—to weigh, though later it also came to be associated with *liberare*—to free or liberate. Both root meanings are pertinent: to live deliberately is to weigh our choices with minds and hearts free of undue influence—to act as free and responsible human beings.

I am blessed in knowing many thoughtful people, but one of them in particular comes to mind when I think of deliberation. When you ask him a question, he pauses to consider; sometimes he stops walking and stands quietly for a moment to think. Sometimes he asks a question to clarify before venturing an opinion. This may sound a bit tedious, but it's actually endearing. For one thing, you know he's giving your question all due consideration, taking it seriously, weighing your words and his own. He also leavens his weighty thoughts with gentle humor and a capacity for irony that becomes any serious truth teller.

Deliberation recognizes the roots and consequences of choice. It takes account of the likely effects of a choice on others and on oneself, of possible complications, of what risks the rewards might merit. When it's a well-practiced habit, all this weighing and foreseeing and measuring and imagining can happen almost instantly. The questions come almost automatically: What will this choice cost in time, energy, money? How will it involve those around me? Others I don't know, but who may be affected? What is likely to change? And if some oppose it, how am I prepared for their opposition? And the wonderful question Quakers raise in response to any invitation life extends: Is this of God?

A dear, funny, wise, and wild woman I have long numbered among my dearest friends has taught me the deep pleasure of deliberation in long conversations, usually on long walks, that open time and space for considering an issue from all sides. She's good at raising unlikely questions. She's also given, now and then, to dropping a sentence that stays with me like an ancient adage. One of these, uttered in an almost offhand way, has provided me with a reliable point of return in my own deliberations over the years: "Every choice you make moves either in the direction of life or in the direction of death."

"Therefore choose life." These simple words from Deuteronomy shine like a pole star among the wide scatterings of circumstance and competing goods that become visible when choice becomes necessary. What is the life-giving choice? The loving one? The one that comes with lightness of being and clarity? Choosing life and choosing it deliberately is a daily practice. It happens in small noticings and quiet, consistent acts of consent to a voice that invites, but doesn't insist, meeting us at every juncture and opening a path.

20

Live Mindfully

"Purity of heart," Soren Kierkegaard famously said, "is to will one thing." That pronouncement didn't make much sense to me when I first heard it. The world, after all, is "vast and beautiful" and there are many things to want and plan and hope for. It took a bit of living before I came to appreciate that "willing one thing" did not mean abstemiously whittling down and excluding, but rather being wholly present—mindful, intentional, and aware—in the moment one is living.

That level of mindfulness can't be maintained without retrieving energies easily scattered by the chronic overstimulation most of us live with. We learn to live with divided hearts and split-level minds as we multi-task. Meditation, centering prayer, or simply finding quiet times and places where we can, as Wendell Berry put it "rest in the grace of the world and be free" are indispensable to the recollection that makes us mindful.

The term has achieved new currency in recent years, perhaps as a response to "mindless" TV shows, vapid entertainment, incessant ads, and soul-killing time-killers. Widely associated with Buddhist teaching of "mindfulness meditation," or *sati*, it has come into common use among people of other faith traditions and people who claim no faith tradition but embrace mindfulness as a way to emotional well-being, mental health and, as has been well tested, physical health.

Any of us who has experienced the blessing of being deeply listened to, given the gift of undivided attention, or witnessed with trust and comprehension knows something of what mindfulness looks like. When we are mindful ourselves, we become more capable of giving that gift of whole presence.

I remember one such gift we received when my step-daughter was dying several years ago: a woman we didn't know showed up at the hospice house and quietly asked if we would allow her simply to sit in meditation by Shona's bedside when we needed to be away for a meal or any other reason. "I feel called to do this," she explained simply. "I just try to be an available, calming presence." Once or twice in the course of our hard days there, we did ask her to come sit, and she came, and sat. She made no particular claims for the efficacy of what she was doing; her gift was simply to be wholly, mindfully present to the mystery we were all witnessing in a young woman's going.

Prayer matters to me, and my understanding of its transformative power is deeply rooted in Christian tradition, itself a rich trove of approaches to the life of the spirit. Mindfulness practices supplement and amplify what I have learned there in ways that have helped open up new avenues of reflection. At their best, both the prayer practices I know and the mindfulness practices I have learned help me in the long learning to "will one thing." I return to that learning again and again because I know that the "pure of heart" are blessed.

21

Live Spaciously

In his fascinating book, *Space, Time and Medicine*, Dr. Larry Dossey explores the way our health is related to how we imagine and occupy space and time. He writes of his work with Native American patients whose understanding of time is more cyclical than linear and how that image of time shapes the way they live into a day or a week or a season.

The notion of time as a line, a road, or a race to a goal imposes its own stress. Cyclical time allows us to relax into the season we're in, knowing it comes with its own gifts, and that other seasons will come in due time with theirs. The liturgical year retains some of the wisdom of the great cycles that continually remind us of recurrence and release. "Modern time," as he calls it, brings with it its own diseases, most related to the stress of feeling driven, locked into schedules that are both tedious and erratic.

Spaciousness is a way of occupying both the times and the spaces we inhabit. One of the people I think of as living spaciously is a woman who lived in small apartment and worked in a small office on a very small budget. But her mind and imagination were wide, her conversation deep and leisurely and laced with wit, and her small table made lovely by an antique cloth and a small vase of flowers. She had many projects afoot and a study full of books and papers, but her home felt like a place where one might "dwell in possibility," welcomed and invited to expand.

A spacious heart says there is enough room. There is enough time. You don't need to suppress what needs to be brought forth, compress what needs to open up, exclude what needs to be included. There is room to explore. There is time to wait for unfolding, to watch the hummingbird hover or the child complete her task.

A small practice that has helped me regain a sense of spaciousness and deepen breath that has been shallowed by a hurried and overcommitted day is to say to myself, instead of "I only have five minutes," "I have *five whole minutes.*" Suddenly, when I pause and do that simple mental exercise, time and space open up a little and I can take a breath, regroup, and return my energies to the moment with more clarity and peace.

Spaciousness of the kind I'm imagining has little to do with the overwrought focus on efficiency that drives so many institutional and personal decisions. It allows one to consider, at least, taking the scenic route rather than the 6-lane freeway; playing on the floor with a child instead of handing him toys and returning to housework; spreading out a project, putting on music, and making the mess required rather than worrying overmuch about what is out of place. Living spaciously is another way of choosing life—a thing we are commanded to do so that our days may be long and our hearts hospitable.

22

Live Kindly

Naomi Shihab Nye's poem "Kindness" speaks of how loss and sorrow are prerequisites to the "tender gravity of kindness"—how kindness comes from empathy with and identification with those who suffer. When you have woken up with sorrow, she writes, when you see how the Indian lying dead by the side of the road could have been you, you can begin to recognize that "it is only kindness that makes sense any more . . . ."

What the poem teaches is that kindness is an attitude and practice that grows from the inside out. We can try to teach children to be kind; we can certainly teach them to be courteous. But all we can really do is to plant the seeds of kindness and nurture them until life offers them its own strenuous lessons that crack those seeds open and release the green shoots.

At its root the word *kind* is related to *kin*. Kindness treats others as kindred—family folk who have a right to our consideration because we are naturally related, of one species. Our needs are the same. Our well-being is dependent in the same way on mutual care. Kindness as what we owe our kin is a tribal idea but extends the tribe to include all who cross our paths. The mere fact of encounter with another human being becomes an invitation and a summoning to awareness: "Oh! You are here too, making your journey on this planet as I am, suffering loss, hoping for help, needing love."

One still occasionally sees the bumper sticker that urges us all to "Practice random acts of kindness." One widespread local response to that invitation happened when drivers at the Oakland Bay Bridge toll booth began to pay tolls for the drivers immediately behind them. As the notion of "random acts of kindness" gained traction, an editor at Conari Press threw a party at which she invited all who attended to tell or write (computers were stationed around the room for the purpose) stories about random acts of kindness in their lives. I was among those honored with an invitation, and I remember it as one of the most remarkable parties I've been to. The book that emerged from it, *Random Acts of Kindness,* is worth reading as an antidote to the steady stream of bad news we've come to expect. Everyone there was celebrating—even reveling in—amazing graces given and received, from small gifts of parking meter money to what seemed angelic appearances in life-threatening moments. That evening kindness came to seem not just a matter of small charitable acts but a powerful and transcendent force, very like what Dylan Thomas called "the force that through the green fuse drives the flower."

In Rick Riordan's *The Battle of the Labyrinth* an older man reminds a younger, "But remember, boy, that a kind act can sometimes be as powerful as a sword." It may be the antidote we most need to the militarism that is wreaking so much destruction. An act of kindness might be what brings us to the tipping point of consciousness that enables us to lay our weapons down and recognize each other as kindred.

23

Live Lightly

The ambiguity is entirely intentional. *Live lightly* in the sense of treading lightly on the earth and its vulnerable life-systems. *Live lightly* in the sense of practicing a "lightness of being" that does not take oneself too seriously, does not weigh the spirit down with old resentments, forgives readily, laughs because the comic dimension is redemptive. *Live lightly* by consenting and learning to be a "light bearer," inhabited and filled by the indwelling Spirit who gives us life.

Simply by being human we are light-bearers. We emit energy. "Vibes" are a real thing. Some people (happily I know a number of them) bring light into any room they enter, subtly, unselfconsciously, probably also unconsciously. In their presence, hearts open and tense muscles relax. It is possible, of course, to hide one's light, not only "under a bushel" but deep within bodies and psyches that are injured, defended, congested by anger, jealousy, or fear.

Living lightly is not possible, for any of us who have made it to adulthood, without some healing. Most of us need in some way to "lighten up." One thing that helps me do that when I find myself (or, these days, my country) in a place of darkness is to carry through the day a word or phrase or sentence from scripture or poetry that redirects me toward the mystery of God's light—physical and metaphysical. I love, for instance the phrase in the Nicene Creed that identifies Christ as "light from light." It brings with it an image of a lightfall cascading downward and outward, covering us with its plumes and mist. It is, for me, an image of abundance and exuberant, life-giving presence.

Or sometimes I find myself hearing and feeling healed by the simple assurance, "I am the light of the world." Christ-light is personal—God with us and around us, immanent and intimate. Or the fact that gives us hope against hope in this bleak midwinter: "The light shines in the darkness, and the darkness has not overcome it."

Living lightly is not only a spiritual practice, but a way of going about daily tasks and entering into ordinary encounters. Sometimes a light touch is all it takes to exchange love or consolation. A light tap on the door can wake a sleeper gently who needs gentleness upon rising. A light once-over may be all it takes to make a house "fair," hospitable, and welcoming. And sometimes a whole morning is made more livable and productive by stopping to watch the sun rise "a ribbon at a time," or to wait at the window just long enough to see a hummingbird alight.

24

Live Harmoniously

I listened this morning to the King's College boy-choir at Cambridge singing the great Christmas hymns that lift me beyond seasonal nostalgia into a wider place of mystery and awe. One began with the bell-like voice of a young boy, his solo amplified and echoing in the great stone chamber of the chapel. After the opening verse others joined him—male voices blended in their particular kind of beauty, supporting that poignant child-sound with rich, full layers of harmony.

Choral music often opens up prayer space for me, partly because it so clearly shows what it means to be "one body." When we pray, we join, as one prayer puts it, "choirs of angels and archangels." We join the "choir invisible" whose membership remains a mystery and whose song is too subtle for human hearing. We join other pilgrim souls who are praying with and for us and sometimes in our stead. We become part of something we did not make and do not control, but which, entered into, brings us home to ourselves in unforeseeable ways.

Our individual work is to find our melody, our line, and sing it. Elie Wiesel writes that at the heart of every story is a song. The earliest human stories, it seems, were songs or poems recited to drumbeats that summoned communities together. Our own stories take shape in the rhythm of daily routine, repetition, recurrence, and recognition of old things made new as consciousness matures and consequences unfold. As those routines involve others, melody finds its way into harmony.

Harmony is not simply a blending of sounds or lines, but also involves tensions held and released—dissonance introduced and then resolved in a return to sounds that complement and comfort. The term comes from a

Greek verb meaning "to fit together." As in a puzzle, fitting involves seeking and finding our place, our partners, our near and distant neighbors, our selves as members, not only as individuals.

Living harmoniously is more than metaphor. We bring the sounds of our voices, the rhythms of our movements, the pace we keep, the energy of our ideas into the places where people gather, and something new emerges at a "vibrational level," if we allow it—if we do not too quickly impose the agendas of the occupied mind. Families or circles of friends, teammates or co-workers who "dwell together in harmony," as the psalmist writes, experience a sensuous delight like "fragrant oil on the head" or "dew . . . that settles on the mountains . . . ." It is "good and pleasant"—modest words for the deep pleasure of security, acceptance, belonging.

The son of one of my dear friends has chosen to work as a choir director. He spends his days helping large assemblies of willing and variously talented people find their way into song. As his hands move, they seem literally to gather and shape the song like a potter at the wheel patiently allowing the clay to take shape under gentle pressure. His leadership is gentle. He opens space and allows others to fill it in a way that helps me understand harmony as a kind of hospitality: we hear and respond to one another as we sing together, making the small adjustments needed until suddenly a chord comes clear and is held in a moment of truth that is its own knowing.

Now, especially, where we experience deep political divisions and dissonance, we need to find the harmonies that align us and enable us to sing "a new song." Melody may be lovely, but it is not enough. There are things we can only know when we know them together. Knowing those things may help us survive.

25

Live Courageously

If, as some of us believe, our country is becoming more militarized, if more people carry guns and feel encouraged to use them, if civil protest is treated as terrorism, if refugees, immigrants and Muslims are targeted for deportation and worse and those who shelter or support them subject to increased surveillance, if more whistleblowers are imprisoned and more prisons are run for profit, even those of us who think we're ordinary, decent, law-abiding citizens and people of good will and good faith may need to tap new veins of courage.

Living a life of faith and moral clarity has always required some measure of courage; the way of the world has always been to protect privilege, marginalize those who threaten the powerful, and scapegoat some to preserve the status quo for others. Jesus warned his followers that they would be persecuted, and they have been, as have Jews and ethnic minorities and people everywhere who have tried to remain faithful to a higher calling than that of power and profit. We need stories of people like Joseph, David, Peter and Paul, the first-century martyrs, of St. Catherine chastising the pope, of Jan Hus praying from the burning stake, of Harriet Tubman and those who ran the Underground Railroad, of women who protected the poor and refused to be disenfranchised, of Maximilian Kolbe and Dietrich Bonhoeffer witnessing from death camp and prison, of Martin Luther King and Gandhi, of the peace teams who show up with supplies in combat zones, of doctors without borders and of the "ordinary" people who occasionally come to public attention for their quiet courage in the face of oppression or ignorance or aggressive fear. Stories are our equipment for living, and we should not go unequipped into the coming decade.

Faith teaches us to live in a larger story than the one woven by news-makers and political pundits or even by historians. It calls us to live not only as rational animals with "enlightened self-interest," but also, and sometimes otherwise, as people whose hearts are capable of widening beyond self-interest and even survival. "What might you be willing to die for?" is a sobering question and clarifying, though I suspect none of us knows what we would actually die for, if put to the test. There are related questions that might be more immediately pertinent: Who needs your protection? Whose efforts, interests, are you willing to support? At what cost? At what risk?

I am under no illusion that I can answer these questions any more courageously than anyone else, nor have my good intentions been put to any very severe tests. I think it's good and right to pray as even Jesus did to let those more severe tests "pass from us," but even as we do, to prepare ourselves for courage by keeping our hearts and eyes wide open. The only real preparation for courage is compassion. And compassion cannot simply be willed; it is a gift given to those who ask from the God of all compassion, who knows our suffering, enters into it, and promises, in the very midst of it, peace and hope that pass understanding.

26

Live Repentantly

If the notion of living repentantly suggests chronic guilt or obsessive self-flagellation, it needs to be redeemed and reclaimed. Repentance has a long and troubled history that has led the scrupulous into thickets of confusing and debilitating guilt. But at its best it is a life-giving habit of mind. Both Catholics and Protestants, as well as many other people of faith, recognize recurrent rituals of repentance as "meet and right" for maintaining spiritual health, right-minded humility, and clarity of intention.

I have long loved these unadorned lines in the General Confession from the *Book of Common Prayer*: "We have erred and strayed in our ways like lost sheep. . . . We have left undone those things which we ought to have done; and we have done those things which we ought not to have done . . . ." That about covers it, and it seems always to be true. It's good to specify what those things are in order to stay mindful and truthful about our own habits and avoid comfortable self-deceptions. (A colleague of mine maintained this mindfulness for himself and the rest of us by attaching a tag at the bottom of every e-mail, Jeremiah's unapologetic reminder: "The heart is deceitful above all things, and desperately wicked.") That sins of commission and omission are part of daily life is a simple truth meant simply to remind us that we are apprentice souls on a learning trajectory that always involves breakage and brokenness and extending and receiving forgiveness. And sheep need a shepherd.

Rituals of repentance, though, however beautifully worded, don't quite get at the inner experience of repentance, which is, I believe, a prerequisite and preparation for the maturing of gratitude. That we receive gifts each day without deserving them—without even knowing to ask for them--that grace does rain down on the just and the unjust from a God who witnesses our struggles with more mercy than we can muster or imagine--are good facts of life to remember. When we think of it widely, in the context of the story of creation, fall, learning, and redemption, a repentant life is one in which we understand more and more deeply how liberally we are blessed and how wonderful it is that no one is keeping score.

Repentant life is a way of living into grace—stepping back to look at ourselves after each failure, betrayal, misbegotten plan or unjust judgment, recognize the need for course correction, and saying thank you for the opportunity to make that correction and the help available as we do it.

Of course repentance involves sorrow. I am, in fact, truly sorry for having hurt those I have hurt. I want to make amends. Twelve-step programs wisely include serious assessment of the damage one has done and serious consideration of how to make amends as part of their recovery program. Part of the wisdom recovery groups impart is insistence upon repentance and amendment as a step toward liberation. Living repentantly frees us from the troubling past and from morbid self-preoccupation to celebrate the freedom and forgiveness that give us back lives worth living, and worth celebrating with the ease and laughter of those who are free, indeed.

27

Live wisely

The way of the wise person, Lao Tzu taught, is the way of water. One translation of the Tao Te Ching puts it this way:

> Nothing is weaker than water,
> But when it attacks something hard
> Or resistant, then nothing withstands it,
> And nothing will alter its way.

Wisdom, he teaches, like water, is fluid, transparent, forceful, shaped by the channels it passes through which it also shapes, reflective, responsive to change in temperature, capable of holding things in solution . . . and so on. The water metaphors that teach us about wisdom are plentiful.

As with much wisdom literature, counterparts to the ancient Chinese text can be found in other traditions. The Hebrew scriptures teach that the wise person is one who listens to God—seeking wisdom from a source beyond himself, beyond the "common sense" of humankind, open to mystery, paradox, transcendence. Wisdom, we read in the stories of David and Solomon and the book of Proverbs, is the defining characteristic of a good leader, who is fair-minded, quick-witted, capable of seeking out and waiting for good counsel, respectful of elders, diligent, humble enough to take correction. In addition to much of this, Muslim tradition teaches that "Wisdom consists in keeping silent, and those who practice it are few." A wise person seeks understanding of the prophet's teachings, and studies how to interpret them.

Jesus' teaching about wisdom both affirms and transcends these widely held notions about what it means to be wise. Directing them to a new level

53

of awareness and understanding, he assured his disciples that something "greater than Solomon" was among them. At twelve he taught his elders in the temple with wisdom "beyond his years," but also confounded them. The Spirit sent to the disciples on Pentecost filled them with a wisdom their adversaries "could not withstand."

Wisdom, it seems, is multifaceted, practical, sometimes bewildering and, perhaps most importantly, open to direction from a Source beyond the rational mind. It pleases me to find that *wise* and *wit* come from the same Germanic root: *wis*. Wit and wisdom have a lot to do with each other. Many of Jesus' encounters with adversaries are witty: he evades their traps and baffles them with riddles (Whose head is on the coin? Would you rescue a sheep on the Sabbath? Who do you say that I am?). Though there is little said about laughter in the Gospels, parables have punch lines of a sort, or reversals that surprise us into reframing and reimagining what goodness and godliness look like.

If we are to live wisely in the times we're given—richly complicated, bewildering, fast-paced, darkened by global threats, challenging to the best minds—we need to pray for and practice the ancient wisdom that will still serve us well, wisdom articulated perhaps best in the Beatitudes, which are not simple teachings but deep, disturbing, paradoxical, heart-opening challenges to "common sense." We need to let ourselves be blessed, made poor in spirit, open to sorrow, humbled, eager for righteousness rather than celebrity. And, like water, willing patiently, in a landscape full of obstacles, to seek and find a way.

28

Live Lovingly

Anne Sexton once wrote of a child, "Love grew around her like crabgrass." It's one of my favorite of her many surprising lines, partly because it makes me smile and remember a particular child, and partly because it gets at something true about love: when it finds a place to take root, it spreads in all directions and finds new places to take root and cling. Love is rooting and branching everywhere—the life force that spins electrons and divides cells and gathers people in smiling, fascinated circles around small children.

A coach I worked with used the expression "in love" more broadly and precisely than most of us who associate it with a particularly besotted state of romantic attraction. When he spoke of a person who worked or played "in love," he seemed to suggest that that person inhabited a particular zone of consciousness or state of awareness, or that love was a kind of weather bubble—a warm place of particular clarity where ambient light gathered. I think of the way he taught me to imagine love when I read Paul's charge to the Ephesians, "Walk in love."

Love, as Reg Presley's song reminds us, is all around, and in our very bodies: "I feel it in my fingers, / I feel it in my toes." Love flows and circulates. We receive it and release it like the breath our lives depend on. From the heart of God it comes to us like light from distant stars, unimaginably swift, burning through cold and darkness.

We are meant and designed to be light-bearers and agents of love. We are invited to dwell in God's love and from that safe place, like a child looking out on the world from the safety of loving arms, to let our own circles of love ripple and widen with every encounter. We are truest to our own nature and most faithful to creation when we live lovingly.

But of course love has, as Virginia Woolf reminds us, a thousand shapes. A thousand faces. A thousand facets, each burning with its own brilliance. Like light, it splays and breaks into discrete colors, some of them dark. Love may be, as St. Paul writes, patient and kind, but it can also be edgy, articulate, able to speak truth to power, fierce with conviction and strong and mysterious as the power of an aikido master.

To live lovingly is to wield a force like a light saber and also to inhabit a force field in which everything is charged with life. And it is to discern prayerfully where and how to call forth that force in the service of the defenseless and the vulnerable. Now more than ever those prayers prepare us for the responsibilities we must take on as bombs are exploded in city streets and lobbed into olive groves where unsuspecting children play.

The great feast of Christmas reminds us of how a vulnerable child came into the world to bear and embody God's own unfathomable love, arriving not in regal majesty, but needing human care, and subject to imperfect, unpracticed human efforts: "Word within a word, unable to speak a word," as T.S. Eliot mysteriously put it. The same love that exploded into galaxies lay sleeping in the arms of a young mother whose consent to his coming represented all human turning toward the Source of all love.

And so we celebrate. And so a thousand Madonnas are adorned and altars bedecked and homes "made fair" and gifts given and the poor more generously gathered and fed this time of year. And we, who wander like sheep into thickets of distraction and sloughs of greed, are brought back into love, reminded, reassured, and released once again like those same sheep who "safely graze," after all, beside streams of living water.

Made in the USA
Monee, IL
09 October 2020